Contents

Oven Temperatures.

	Farenheit	Gas	Celsius
Slow	300	2	150
	325	3	170
Moderate	350	4	180
	375	5	190
	400	6	200
Hot	425	7	220
	450	8	230

Weights

Avoirdupois	Metric
1oz	29.5grms
4oz	115grms, approx.
8oz	220 " "
1 lb	454 " "

Liquid Measures

Imperial	Metric
1 teaspoon	8 millilitres approx.
1 tablespoon	20 " "
1 fl. oz	30 " "
1/4 pt	145 " "
1/2 pt	285 " "
1 pt	570 " "

1000 millilitres = 1 litre.

Rosemary's guide to Shopping on a budget

If you find your income has reduced and you have to be more selective when shopping, plan your shopping wisely. Look out for bargains and ask for discount. Make a list before you go and remember when you buy raw food, you may also need the items to cook it with. To prepare a nutritious well balanced diet you do not require a large amount of expensive meat, fish or exotic vegetables. Pasta or rice with a cheese sauce and vegetables make a substantial main course. Select the supermarket with special offers and where you deem foods to be cheaper than other stores. When shopping in the supermarket buy the stores own brand items, many of which are of excellent quality and are much cheaper than regular items. Fresh vegetables and fruit in season will be cheaper. Buy only what you need. Do not go shopping in haste, If you do, you may spend more than your budget allows. And finally leave the credit card at home.

Soups

Nettle Soup

Ingredients

8ozs, 220g Potatoes (diced)

2 Parsnips (diced)

2 Onions (diced)

6ozs, 175g Young nettles
(chopped)

2 tablespoons Pearl barley.

1 Chicken stock cube.

1 Litre Water.

Salt and freshly ground pepper.

2ozs, 60g Butter/Margarine.

4 tablespoons Cream.

Method

Melt the butter in the saucepan. When melted add the potatoes, onion and parsnip. Cover and sweat on a gentle heat until the onions are soft. Dissolve the stock cube in the water and add it to the vegetables, bring to the boil and simmer until the vegetables are cooked. Add the chopped nettles and season to taste. Simmer for a few minutes and add the cream. Serve hot.

Chicken Soup

Ingredients

1 Chicken carcass.	1 Litre of water.
2 Onions (chopped)	Salt and freshly ground black pepper.
2 Carrots (diced)	2 tablespoons of chopped parsley.
2 Sticks of celery (finely chopped)	

1 teaspoon of mixed herbs.

Method

Remove the chicken meat from the carcass, mince and put it in a saucepan. Add the water, vegetables and mixed herbs. Cover, bring to the boil and simmer gently for 20 minutes or until the vegetables are soft. Remove the saucepan from the heat, skim the fat from the top and season to taste. Add the parsley and continue to simmer uncovered for a further 15 minutes. Serve hot.

Mutton Broth

Ingredients

8ozs, 220g lean neck of
Mutton (minced)

2 Carrots (diced)	8ozs, 220g Potatoes (diced)
1 white turnip (diced)	1 tablespoon pearl barley.
3 Onions (diced)	1 tablespoon parsley (chopped)
1 litre Water.	1 teaspoon of mixed herbs.

Method

Put all the vegetables except the parsley in a pot. Add the meat, mixed herbs and pearl barley. Cover with water and bring to the boil. Simmer gently for 1 hour. Remove from the heat and skim the fat from the top. Season to taste. Add the parsley and simmer gently for a few minutes. Serve hot.

Potato and Onion Soup

Ingredients

8ozs, 220g potatoes (diced)   2ozs,60g Butter or margarine.

4 Onions (finely chopped)   1 chicken stock cube.

1 litre water.   Salt and pepper to taste.

1 tablespoon of chopped parsley.

Method

Put the butter in the saucepan on a low heat. Add the onions and sweat until clear. Add the potatoes and season to taste. Pour in the water and bring to the boil. Reduce the heat, cover and simmer for 30 minutes. Stir in the chopped parsley and serve hot.

Mushroom Soup

Ingredients

1 lb, 454g Mushrooms (chopped)	2ozs, 60g Butter or margarine.
2 Onions (finely chopped)	1 chicken stock cube.
Salt and freshly ground black pepper.	2ozs,60g flour.
1/2 litre Milk.	1/2 litre water.

Method

Melt the butter in the saucepan. Add the onion, cover and sweat over a gentle heat until soft. Put in the mushrooms and simmer gently for 5 minutes. Stir in the flour, cook for 3 minutes and season to taste. Dissolve the stock cube in the water and pour over the mushrooms stirring all the time. Gradually add the milk, increase the heat and bring to the boil. Simmer for 5 minutes. Serve hot.

Mixed Vegetable

Ingredients

2 Carrots (diced)

2 Parsnips (finely chopped)

1oz butter or margarine.

1 litre Water. Salt and freshly ground pepper.

1 vegetable stock cube.

1 tablespoon of parsley (chopped)

2 sticks celery (finely chopped)

2 Onions (finely sliced)

1oz, 30g Flour.

1 bay leaf.

1 teaspoon mixed herbs.

Method

Melt the butter in the saucepan and add the vegetables. Cook gently, stirring occasionally. Dissolve the stock cube in the water and pour over the vegetables. Add the mixed herbs and the bay leaf. Put on the lid and bring to the boil. Reduce the heat and simmer gently for 30 minutes. Blend the flour with a little water and add to the soup. Mix well and simmer for a few minutes. Sprinkle with chopped parsley.

Serve hot

Budget meals for 4 costing only €4 to make

Minced Lamb Pie

Ingredients

8ozs, 220g Minced breast of lamb.

2 Onions (diced)	2 tablespoons of oil.
2 Carrots (diced)	1/4, 145ml of water.
2 Papsnips (diced)	1 stock cube.

Method

Put some oil on the pan and fry the onion until soft add the minced lamb and fry until brown stirring all the time. Blend the stock cube in the water and add to the meat then add the vegetables. Bring to the boil and simmer for 5 minutes transfer to a pie dish.

Ingredients for pastry

6ozs, 235g Flour.	2ozs, 60g Margarine.
1/2 teaspoon Baking powder.	1 table spoon of water.

Method

Sieve the flour and baking powder into a bowl, rub in the margarine and add the water. Mix to form a dough. Shake some flour on to a board and roll out to the size of the pie dish you are using. Use about 2/3 to line the dish and put in the mixture from the pan. Roll out the remaining pastry and cover the dish. Bake in a hot oven 200°C, 400°F, Gas 6 for 35 minutes or until pastry is golden brown.

Vegetable Hot - pot

Ingredients

8 Potatoes (sliced)	2 Onions (sliced)
3ozs, 90g Cabbage (shredded)	2 Parsnips (sliced)
3 Carrots (sliced)	3 Sticks of celery (chopped)
1 Stock cube.	

Method

Arrange the potato and vegetables in layers in a lightly greased pie dish finishing with a layer of potato.

Melt the stock cube in water and add to the dish, almost covering the vegetables, cover and place in the oven at 190°C, 375°F, Gas 5, for one hour or until vegetables are tender.

Suggestion

When boiling cabbage, cauliflower or steaming fish. Add some sliced onion. This prevents any un-wanted smells going through the house.

Tripe and Onions with Pasta.

Ingredients

1lb 454g Tripe.	1/2lb 220g Onions (chopped)
1 litre Milk.	1 stock cube.
1 lb, 454g Pasta.	1 tablespoon Parsley (chopped)
1 tablespoon of corn flour.	

Salt and freshly ground black pepper.

Method

Put the tripe in a saucepan with the milk and chopped onions and simmer for 1 hour or until tender, then remove the tripe from the saucepan and cut into strips about 1" long. Put the pasta in a saucepan of boiling water, add a teaspoon of oil and simmer for 10 minutes. Dissolve the cornflour and stock cube in a little milk and add to the saucepan with the milk and onions, bring to the boil stirring all the time until thick and creamy. Add the tripe and pasta, season to taste and mix well. Garnish with chopped parsley.

Meat Balls and Croquette Potato with Baked Beans

Ingredients:

1/2 lb,220g cold meat (minced)

2 lb,908g potatoes(peeled)

1 Onion (finely chopped)

1 teaspoon of mixed herbs (dried or fresh)

3 tablespoons of Bread crumbs.

1 Egg (beaten)

1 Tin of beans.

1 tablespoon of chopped parsley.

2 tablespoon of flour.

Method:

Put the potatoes into a saucepan of boiling water and simmer for 30 minutes or until cooked. Drain, mash and allow to cool. Break the egg into a small bowl and whisk. Put the mince, onion, herbs and half the mashed potato into a large bowl and mix well. Shake some flour on to your hands and form the mixture into balls. Put the bread crumbs into a bowl. Coat the meat balls with egg, then bread crumbs and fry in a pre-heated fat fryer until golden brown. Then form the remaining mashed potatoes into rolls coat with egg and bread crumbs and fry in the fat fryer. When done remove and place on absorbent paper to soak excess oil. Garnish with parsley. Remove the baked beans from the tin and heat. Serve with the meatballs and croquettes potatoes.

Spaghetti with Tomato Sauce

Ingredients

14ozs, 400g Spaghetti.   3 Onions (finely chopped)

1 Tin of Tomatoes (chopped)   1/2 Clove of garlic (crushed)

1 Tablespoon of oil.   2 Tablespoons of tomato sauce.

Salt and freshly ground black pepper.

Method:

Put the spaghetti in a large pot of boiling water. Add a teaspoon of oil and boil for 10 minutes until tender. When cooked, drain and place in a serving dish , keep hot. Put some oil on the pan and add the onion and garlic, fry until soft. Add the tinned tomatoes with juice and the tomato sauce. Season to taste. Simmer for about 10 minutes stirring all the time. Remove from the heat and pour over the spaghetti.

Suggestion

To peel tomatoes: Prick them with a fork and put them in a bowl. Pour boiling water over them and leave for 1 minute. Then strip off the skins.

Grilled Sausages, Carrots and Rustic Chips.

Ingredients

8oz, 220g Sausages .

4 Large Potatoes,

1 lb, 454g Carrots.

1 tablespoon of oil.

Method:

Put the carrots in a saucepan of boiling water and cook for 15 minutes, drain and keep hot. Brush the grill with a little oil and place the sausages on it. Grill on all sides until cooked and a brown colour. Wash and slice the potatoes chip size leaving the skins on. put in a pre-heated fat fryer until golden brown, remove and place on tissue paper to absorb the excess oil. Serve with the sausages and carrots.

Did you know?

Fats and starches insulate the body against heat loss and provide energy. They are found in animal fats, fish oil, vegetable oil, milk, cheese, butter, nuts and margarine.

Lambs Kidneys, Tomato and Mashed Potato

Ingredients

4 Lambs Kidneys(skin removed)

1 lb, 445g Potatoes, (peeled)

2 tablespoons of oil.

1 clove of garlic (crushed)

1 tablespoon of flour.

2 Onions (sliced)

4 Tomatoes
(skinned and sliced)

1 tablespoon tomato
puree.

Method:

Put the potatoes in a pot of boiling water and boil for about 30 minutes or until cooked. When cooked drain, mash and season to taste. Transfer to a serving dish and keep hot. Put some oil on the frying pan, put on the kidneys and fry briskly until brown, reduce the heat and continue to simmer for about 10 minutes. Remove the kidneys from the pan and slice. Put the sliced onion and garlic on the pan and fry until soft. Dissolve the stock cube in a cup of water and add the tomato puree and flour. Mix well and pour on to the pan. Add the kidneys and simmer gently for 5 minutes stirring occasionally. Add the sliced tomato to the pan and serve with the mashed potato.

Egg Salad with Boiled Potatoes

Ingredients

1lb,450g Potatoes.	1/2 Cucumber (sliced)
4 Eggs.	4 tablespoons of mayonnaise.
1 Lettuce, washed.	1/4 teaspoon paprika.
4 Tomatoes (sliced)	1 Onion (finely chopped)

Method:

Put the eggs in a saucepan of cold water and bring to the boil. Simmer for 10 minutes, then plunge them into cold water at once to prevent a dark line forming around the yolk. Put the potatoes in a saucepan of boiling water, bring to the boil and simmer for 30 minutes or until cooked, drain and put in a serving dish. Remove the shells and halve the eggs lengthways. Mix together the mayonnaise and chopped onion and season to taste. Arrange lettuce leaves on each of four individual plates. Top the lettuce with two egg halves, spoon the mayonnaise on top and sprinkle with paprika. Arrange the sliced tomato and cucumber around the eggs. Serve with the potatoes.

Fried Eggs with Crispy Potatoes and Cabbage

Ingredients:

8 potatoes,   3 tablespoons of oil.

4 Eggs. 1 small onion (sliced)   1 Head of spring cabbage (shredded)

Method:

Peel and boil the potatoes whole in a saucepan of boiling water for 15 minutes. Drain, cool and slice evenly. Fry on the pan in the oil until crisp and golden. Transfer to a serving dish and keep hot. Put the shredded cabbage in a pot with boiling water and add the sliced onion. Boil for 10 minutes or until tender. When cooked drain, chop, put in a serving dish and keep hot. Put some oil on a frying pan and break the eggs individually on to the pan and cook slowly spooning the oil over the eggs until a thin white film forms over the yolk. Serve with the fried potatoes and cabbage.

Braised Lambs Hearts with Mashed Potatoes.

Ingredients:

4 Lambs hearts (trimmed with centres removed)

1 stock cube	1 table spoon of flour.
2 Onion s(chopped)	1 tablespoon of oil.
1 Clove of garlic (crushed)	1/2 litre Water.

1lb, 454g Potatoes (peeled)

For herb stuffing:

4 tablespoons of fresh bread crumbs.

1 tablespoon of mixed herbs (fresh or dried)

1 egg beaten.

Method:

Put the bread crumbs and herbs in a bowl add the beaten egg to moisten and mix well. Fill the centre of the hearts with the stuffing and sew up the opening with fine string or thread. Put some oil on the pan, add the hearts and simmer gently until brown on all sides, take them out of the pan and put in the chopped onions and garlic and cook until soft. Transfer the onions, garlic and hearts to a roasting dish, Dissolve the stock cube in the 1/2 litre of water and season to taste. Braise in the oven at 180°C, 350°F Gas 4 for 1 hour or until tender. Put the potatoes in a pot of water, bring to the boil and simmer for 30 minutes or until cooked. When cooked, drain, mash, put in a serving dish and keep hot. Remove the hearts from the oven and slice them. Thicken the liquid with the flour and pour over the hearts. Serve with mashed potato.

Did you know ?

Vitamins and salts are necessary for growth and health. They are found in spinach, broccoli, cabbage, potatoes, root vegetables, fruit, milk, cheese, eggs, meat, poultry,fish, nuts, whole grain bread, liver, cereals, yeast, peas, beans etc.

Vegetarian Stir-Fry
with Spaghetti

Ingredients:

12oz, 335g Spaghetti.	2 Onions (chopped)
2 Sticks of celery (finely chopped)	2 tomatoes (chopped)
2 tablespoons tomato puree.	2ozs Cabbage (shredded)
1 table spoon of oil.	1 Green pepper (sliced)
1 cup of stock.	1 clove of garlic (crushed)

Salt and freshly ground black pepper.

Method:

Put the spaghetti in a large pot of water, add a teaspoon of oil and simmer gently for 10 minutes or until tender, stirring occasionally. Drain well, transfer to a serving dish and keep hot. Put the oil on the frying pan or wok and heat. When hot add the sliced onion and garlic. Fry until clear, then add the celery, pepper, cabbage, tomato and the cup of stock. Cook gently for about 8 minutes. Add the sauce, season to taste, mix well and fry for a further 5 minutes. Pour on to the dish with the cooked spaghetti and serve.

Baked Stuffed Potatoes and Cabbage.

Ingredients

4 Large potatoes.

4oz, 120g Minced meat. cheese.

1 head of cabbage (shredded)

3 Onions (finely chopped)

2 tablespoons of oil. 2oz Grated cheese.

1/4 teaspoon paprika.

Method:

Prick the potatoes, brush with oil and bake in a hot oven. Put the cabbage in a saucepan with some of the chopped onion and add enough boiling water to half cover the cabbage. Bring to the boil and simmer for 10 minutes. Drain, chop, put in a serving dish and keep hot. Put some oil on the frying pan add the minced meat, onion and carrot, fry for about 10 minutes or until the meat is fully cooked, stirring occasionally. Season to taste and stir well. When the potatoes are cooked, drain them and leave to cool slightly for a few minutes. Cut a thin slice off the flat side of the potatoes and with a teaspoon scoop out the centre and put it on a plate. Remove as much of the potato as possible without breaking the skin. Add the scooped out potato mash to the mince, carrot and onion mixture and mix well. Fill the potato shells with this mixture and sprinkle the grated cheese on top. Place in a hot oven at 200°C, 400°F, Gas 6 for 20 minutes or until golden brown. Serve with the cabbage.

Fried Eggs with Tomatoes and Potato Cakes.

Ingredients

4oz, 115g flour.	8oz, 220g cooked mashed potatoes.
2oz, 60g Butter.	1 teaspoon of baking powder.
2 table spoons of oil.	4 Tomatoes, cut in quarters.
4 Eggs.	Pepper and salt.

Method:

Sieve together the flour, baking powder and seasoning into a bowl and rub in the butter. Work in the mashed potatoes to form a dough and roll out on to a floured board, cut into rounds and fry on a lightly oiled pan, turn, and fry until golden brown. Remove on to a dish and keep hot. Add a little oil to the frying pan and break the eggs individually on to it. Simmer for a few minutes spooning the oil over the yolk of each of the eggs until the eggs are covered in a white film. Add the tomatoes and fry for a few minutes. Remove and serve with the potato cakes and eggs.

Vegetable Curry with Rice

Ingredients:

14oz, 400g Long grain rice.   2 Onions(chopped.)

1 clove of garlic (crushed)   1 teaspoon of curry powder.

2 Apples   1 Stock cube (dissolved in water)
(cored and chopped)

2 Carrots (chopped).   3-4 pepper corns (crushed)

1 Green pepper   2 tablespoons of oil
(de-seeded and chopped)

2 sticks of celery (finely chopped) .

Method:

Boil the rice in a saucepan of boiling water add a few
drops of oil and simmer for 30 minutes, drain and put in a
serving dish. Keep hot. Heat the oil in a frying pan and
add the onion and garlic, fry until soft. Transfer to the
saucepan with the carrot, apple, pepper and celery. Add
the stock with enough water to cover the vegetables. Stir
in the curry powder and crushed pepper corns and bring to
the boil. Reduce the heat and simmer gently for 45
minutes. Serve on a bed of rice.

Braised Lambs Liver with Mushrooms and Boiled Potatoes.

Ingredients

8 Potatoes, peeled.

1/2 lb, 220g Lambs liver, sliced.

1/2 lb, 220g Mushrooms.

2 oz, 60mls oil.

Salt and pepper.

1 oz, 3oz Butter.

2 Onions, chopped.

1 oz, 30g Flour.

4 oz, 120mls Water or stock.

1 stock cube.

Method:

Put the potatoes in a pot of boiling water bring to the boil and simmer for about 30 minutes or until cooked. Drain, place in a serving dish and keep hot. Meanwhile heat a little oil in a saucepan, add the sliced onions and sliced mushrooms and cook for 2-3 minutes. Add the stock or water and cover. Cook for a further 10 minutes. Remove from the heat, place in a serving dish and keep hot. Sift the flour, pepper and salt on to a plate and roll the slices of liver in this. Melt the butter in a frying pan, put in the liver and fry on both sides for 2-3 minutes. Remove from the heat and add to the dish with the mushrooms and onion. Serve with the potatoes.

Tomato and Egg with Rice

Ingredients

4 Large tomatoes	14oz, 400g Long grain rice.
4 Eggs.	Pepper and salt.
2 Onions, finely chopped.	1 teaspoon mixed herbs.
4oz 115g bread crumbs.	2 tablespoons of oil.
1 tablespoon water.	1 tablespoon of chopped parsley.

Method:

Put the rice in a saucepan of boiling water add a couple of drops of oil and boil for 30 minutes or until soft. Drain and put in a serving dish, keep hot. Meanwhile put some oil in the frying pan, add the chopped onions and fry until clear. Transfer to a bowl and add the bread crumbs, mixed herbs and the water. Mix well. Cut the top off the tomatoes. scoop out the centres, chop and add this to the bread crumb mixture and mix well. Break a raw egg into each of the tomato shells and spoon the crumb mixture on top. Place the tomatoes on a baking tray and bake in the oven at 180°C, 350°F, Gas 4 for 15 minutes. remove from oven sprinkle with chopped parsley and serve on a bed of rice.

Parsnip and Sausage Bake

Ingredients:

1lb, 454g Potatoes, peeled.   3 Parsnips, peeled.

8 Pork Sausages.   2 Onions, peeled.

1oz, 30mls Oil.   1 tsp of mixed herbs.

Method:

Cut the peeled potatoes, onion and parsnips into slices of equal thickness and place in a casserole dish in alternate layers. Season with mixed herbs. Add sufficient water to cover the vegetables. Place in the oven at 180°C, 350°F, Gas 4 for 30 minutes. Put some oil on the pan and fry the sausages until golden brown. Remove the casserole from the oven and place the sausages in rows on top. Return the casserole to the oven for a further 10 minutes.

Spaghetti Carbonara

Ingredients:

2 Filleted pieces of Whiting.

14oz, 400g Pasta.

2 Onions (sliced)

1/2 Litre milk.

1 vegetable stock cube.

2 Tomatoes, sliced.

2oz, 60g Grated cheese.

2 tablespoons oil.

Salt and freshly ground black pepper.

2ozs, 60g Flour.

Method:

Put the pasta in a saucepan of boiling water add a teaspoon of oil and boil for 10 minutes. Cut the fish into 1" size pieces and remove any bones that may remain there after filleting. Place in a saucepan and cover with cold water. Bring to the boil and simmer for 5 minutes. Remove from the pan and drain, reserve the fish stock and crumble in the stock cube stirring until dissolved. Put some oil on the pan and fry the onion until soft, stir in the flour and cook for 1 minute. Season to taste and blend in the reserved fish stock, bring to the boil stirring all the time until thickened. Add the cooked fish and pasta, mixing well. Pour into a lightly greased casserole dish. Sprinkle the grated cheese on top and add the slices of tomato. Cook in a pre-heated oven 180°C, 350°F. gas 4 for about 15 minutes.

Champ

Ingredients

8-10 Potatoes.

1 small bunch scallions (chopped)

1 litre Milk.

4ozs,115g Butter or Margarine.

Salt and freshly ground black pepper.

Method

Put the potatoes in a pot of boiling water, Bring to the boil and simmer for 30 minutes or until cooked. Put the milk in a saucepan. Add the chopped scallions. Bring to the boil and simmer for 3 minutes. Turn off the heat and leave to infuse. Drain, peel and mash the boiled potatoes. Add the boiling milk and onions, Season to taste and add some butter if desired. Mix well and serve with a knob of butter melting in the centre.

Spaghetti Bolognese

Ingredients:

8oz, 230g of Minced meat.	2 Onions, chopped.
14oz, 400g Spaghetti.	1 Tin of tomatoes.
1 clove of garlic (crushed)	Freshly ground black pepper.
2oz, 60mls Oil.	2 tablespoons of bolognese sauce or tomato puree.

Method:

Put the spaghetti in a large saucepan of boiling water, Add 1 teaspoon of oil and bring to the boil and simmer for about 10 minutes stirring occasionally. Remove from the heat and transfer to a serving dish and keep hot. Put oil in the frying pan, add the onion and garlic, cook until soft, then add the mince and tomatoes and simmer until the meat is thoroughly cooked. Add the bolognese or tomato sauce and mix well. Season to taste and simmer for 10 minutes. Pour over the cooked spaghetti and serve.

Lasagne

Ingredients:

12ozs, 335g Minced beef.	1 tablespoon of oil.
4ozs, 220g lasagne.	1 beef stock cube.
2 Onion (chopped)	2 tablespoons tomato puree.
3oz grated cheese.	1/2litre Water.
Salt and pepper.	

Method:

Put the oil on the frying pan and fry the onion until clear. Add the minced beef and fry for 5 minutes until brown. Dissolve the stock cube in the water, add the tomato puree, mix well and pour on to the pan. Season to taste and bring to the boil, reduce the heat and gently simmer for 10 minutes, stirring occasionally. Remove from the pan and spread a layer of the mixture on the base of a lightly greased baking dish, followed by a layer of lasagne, continue layering until the mixture is used up. Top with the grated cheese. Bake in a pre-heated oven200°C, 400°F, Gas 6 for about 30 minutes or until cooked.

Potato Cakes with Baked Beans

Ingredients

4oz, 115g Flour.

8oz, 220g Cooked
mashed potatoes.

1 teaspoon of baking powder.

1/2 teaspoon of mixed herbs.

1 tin baked beans.

2oz 60g Butter.

1 tablespoon of oil

Salt and pepper.

3oz, 90mls Milk.

Method

Sieve together the flour, baking powder and seasoning into
the bowl of mashed potato. Sprinkle in the herbs. Add the
butter and milk and mix well to form a dough. Put the
dough on a floured board and roll out, cut into shape and
fry on a lightly oiled pan until golden brown, turn and fry
the other side the same. Open the tin of beans put in a
saucepan and heat for a few minutes. Serve with the
potato cakes.

Cauliflower Cheese

Ingredients

1 Large Cauliflower.

4ozs, 115g grated cheese.

1 Onion (chopped)

3 table spoons of fresh bread crumbs.

2oz, 60g melted butter.

Method:

Break the cauliflower into florets and put in a pot of boiling water and boil for 15minutes with the chopped onion. Drain and put in a lightly greased baking dish. Put the cheese and bread crumbs into a bowl, add the melted butter and mix well. Sprinkle this mixture over the cauliflower and bake in the oven at 180°C, 350°f Gas 4 for 10 minutes or until the topping is golden brown.

Mackerel with Carrots and Boiled Potatoes.

Ingredients:

4 pieces of Mackerel.

8 Potatoes, peeled.

1lb Carrots (sliced)

1 Lemon, sliced.

2 Tomatoes, sliced.

1 tablespoon of parsley, chopped.

2 Tablespoons oil.

Method:

Put the potatoes in a saucepan of boiling water and boil for 30 minutes. Remove from the heat, drain, put in a serving dish and keep hot. Put the carrots in a saucepan with enough water to cover them and boil for 15 minutes, drain and keep hot. Put a little oil on the pan and add the fish pieces. Fry gently for about 5 minutes, turn and fry for a further 5 minutes. Remove from the pan and garnish with the sliced tomato and lemon. Drain and serve with the carrots and potatoes.

Stir- fried Sweet and Sour Chicken.

Ingredients:

2 Chicken boneless breasts
(finely sliced)

2 tablespoons of oil.

1 Tablespoon soy sauce.

1 Onion (chopped)

1 Green pepper
(deseeded and sliced

)2 Carrots (grated)

1 Clove of garlic (crushed)

1 teaspoon brown sugar.

1/4 litre Chicken stock.

1 teaspoon of root ginger.

Salt and freshly ground black pepper.

14ozs,400g Pasta.

Method:

Heat some oil in the wok and add the chicken pieces. Stir-fry for 8-10 minutes, or until golden brown. Remove and place in a dish and keep warm. Put the onions, and garlic in the wok and fry until clear. Add the broccoli, carrots and green pepper and fry for 5 minutes. Mix together the chicken stock, brown sugar and soy sauce. Pour into the wok. Sprinkle on the ginger, black pepper and salt to taste. Simmer for 3 minutes, add the cooked chicken and simmer for a further 3 minutes. Meanwhile put the pasta in a saucepan of boiling water. Add a teaspoon of oil and simmer for 10 minutes or until cooked.

Tripe and Vegetable Casserole with Boiled Potatoes

Ingredients:

1 lb, 454g Tripe
(cut into small pieces)

2 Celery sticks
(finely chopped)

2 Parsnips (chopped)

1 stock cube.
2 Carrots (chopped)

1 1/2 Litres of water.
1 lb, 454g Potatoes (peeled)

1 Leek, washed, trimmed, split
lengthwise and finely chopped.

Method:

Put the tripe in a saucepan of water and boil for 30
minutes, drain and transfer to the casserole dish with the
chopped carrots, parsnips leek and celery. Dissolve the
stock cube in sufficient water to cover the vegetables,
cover and place in the oven for 30 minutes or until the
vegetables are soft and the tripe is cooked. Meanwhile put
the potatoes into a saucepan of boiling water and boil for
30 minutes or until cooked. Drain and place in a serving
dish. Sprinkle some parsley over them and keep hot.
Remove the tripe and vegetables from the oven when
cooked add the chopped parsley. Pour into a serving dish
and serve with the boiled potatoes.

Chicken Cakes with Grilled Tomatoes

Ingredients:

8oz, 220g of cooked chicken (minced)

1 Egg (beaten)

1lb,454g mashed potatoes.

2ozs, 60g Fresh bread crumbs.

1 onion (finely chopped)

1 teaspoon of mixed herbs

2ozs Flour.

(fresh or dried)

1/2 lb, 220g Tomatoes.

Pepper and salt.

Method:

Put all the ingredients into a bowl and mix well. Flour your hands and form the mixture into small round cakes about 1" in thickness. Coat them with the beaten egg and roll them in bread crumbs. Put them in the pre-heated fat fryer and cook through until they are brown in colour. Remove and place on absorbent paper to absorb the excess oil. Meanwhile Cut the tomatoes in half and place on a lightly greased grill rack and place under a pre-heated grill for 5-8 minutes. Serve with the chicken cakes.

Egg Mayonnaise with Sardines and Green Leaf Salad

Ingredients:

4 Eggs

1 tin of sardines.

1 Head of Lettuce.

1/4 teaspoon paprika

1 tablespoon chopped chives

4 table spoons mayonnaise

2 Tomatoes (sliced)

Salt and pepper.

2 teaspoons lemon juice

Method

Hard boil the eggs for 10 minutes, then plunge them into cold water at once to prevent a dark line forming around the yolk. Remove the shells and halve the eggs lengthways. Open the tin of sardines, drain, trim, shred and put in a bowl. Add the mayonnaise, cream, lemon juice and seasoning and mix well. Arrange the green salad leaves on each of four individual plates. Top the lettuce with two egg halves and the shredded sardines in mayonnaise. Garnish each with sliced tomato and a sprinkling of chopped chives and serve with brown home made bread.

Onion and Bacon Roly Poly

Ingredients:

4 Rashers of bacon (rind removed)

4 oz, 115g Margarine.

4oz, 115g Cheese (grated)

2 large Onions (peeled and sliced)

4oz, 115g Self-raising flour.

1 tablespoon of oil.

Salt and pepper. Water to mix.

1 teaspoon of baking powder.

1 Egg (beaten)

1 teaspoon of mixed herbs.

Method:

Sieve the flour, baking powder and mixed herbs into a mixing bowl and season to taste. Rub in the margarine with your fingertips and add sufficient water to make a dough. Remove the dough from the bowl and place on a floured surface and roll out to a rectangular shape. Put some oil on the pan and fry the onions and bacon in the oil until cooked, remove and allow to cool.When cool cut the rashers into fine strips and spread them with the onions over the rolled out pastry. Sprinkle over the grated cheese. Brush the edges of the pastry with the beaten egg and roll up like a swiss roll and seal the ends. Make diagonal cuts across the top.Place on a lightly floured baking tray and bake in the oven at 200°C, 400°F, gas 6 for about one hour until golden brown.

Savoury Omelette with Rustic Chips

Ingredients (for one)   **Make 4.**

2 Eggs

1 tablespoon of milk.

Salt and pepper

1 tablespoon of chopped parsley.

2 tablespoons of oil.

4 large potatoes (cut into chips)

Method:

Put the chips in the pre heated deep fat fryer and cook until golden brown. Remove, place in a serving dish and keep hot. Separate the yolks from the whites of the eggs, mix the milk, yolks, salt, pepper and parsley together. Beat the whites to a froth and pour the yolks on to the whites and mix lightly together. Put a little oil on to a small frying pan, pour in the omelete mix and cook until it begins to set. Check if the bottom of the omelette is brown by lifting slightly at the edges. When cooked, fold in two and serve immediately.

Macaroni Cheese

Ingredients:

14oz, 400g Macaroni.	50g butter
2oz 60g plain flour	1 litre of milk
6oz 175g grated cheese	Salt and pepper
1 teaspoon of mixed herbs.	

Method

Put the macaroni into a large saucepan of boiling water add 1 teaspoon of oil and simmer gently for 30 minutes or until tender, drain and set aside. Melt the butter in a saucepan over a low heat, add the flour and cook for 2 minutes, add the milk gradually, stirring all the time bring to the boil. Simmer gently for 2-3 minutes. Remove from the heat and season with mixed herbs. Add the cooked macaroni and 150g of the cheese to the sauce and mix well. Pour the mixture into a serving dish and sprinkle the remaining cheese over the top. Brown under a hot grill and serve immediately.

Chicken Wings on a Bed of Rice

Ingredients:

14oz, 400g Long grain rice. 2 Onions (diced)

1/2 lb, 220g Chicken wings. 1 stock cube.

4oz, 115g Mushrooms   1/4 teaspoon of ground ginger.
(chopped)

2 Sticks of celery   Salt and freshly ground pepper.
(finely chopped)

3 tablespoons of oil.

Method:

Put the rice in a saucepan of water and add one teaspoon
of oil. Bring to the boil, cover and reduce the heat.
Simmer for about 30 minutes or until the rice is cooked
and the water has been absorbed. Transfer to a serving
dish. Fluff up the rice with a fork and keep hot.
Meanwhile put some oil on the pan and fry the chopped
onion until soft. Add the chicken wings and fry until
brown. Transfer to a casserole dish, add the diced
vegetables. Blend the ground ginger and stock cube in 1
litre of water. Season to taste and add to the dish. Put the
casserole dish in the pre-heated oven and cook for 30
minutes at 190°C, 375°F, gas 5. When cooked remove and
serve with the rice.

Hamburgers with Tomato and Lettuce.

Ingredients:

3/4lb, 335g Lean minced beef.

1/4 lb,115g fresh bread crumbs.

1/2 teaspoon mixed herbs.

1 Egg (beaten)

2oz, 60g Flour.

Salt and pepper.

2 tomatoes (sliced)

2 Onions Sliced.

4 hamburger buns.

1 head of lettuce.

Method:

Put the minced beef, bread crumbs, mixed herbs and beaten egg in a bowl. Mix well and season to taste. With your hands remove the mixture, form into a ball and place on a well floured board. Shake some flour over it and roll out to about 1/4"thickness, cut into rounds and place on a lightly greased grill rack. Put them under the pre-heated grill.Grill for 5 minutes on each side or until the hamburgers are well browned. Reduce the heat and cook for a further 5 minutes on either side. Serve on split hamburger buns with onion rings, tomato and lettuce.

Savoury Rice

Ingredients:

14oz, 400g Long grain Rice.

4oz, 115g Mushrooms(sliced)

1 tin of Tomatoes, chopped.

2 Onions (sliced)

1/2 teaspoon mixed herbs.

1 Green pepper
(de-seeded and chopped)

1 Red pepper
(de-seeded and finely
chopped)

1 garlic clove (crushed)

3 tablespoons of oil.

1/4 teaspoon of crushed
black pepper.

Method:

Put the rice in a saucepan of hot water and add 1 teaspoon
of oil. Bring to the boil and simmer for 30 minutes or until
cooked. In a large frying pan put some oil and place over
a moderate heat. Add the onions and garlic and fry until
soft. Then add the green and red peppers, tomatoes with
the juice from the tin, mushrooms, black pepper and
mixed herbs. Mix well and cook for 5-10 minutes stirring
occasionally. Drain the rice and add to the pan. Mix very
well and cook for a further 3- 5 minutes, stirring all the
time. Transfer to a serving dish and serve.

Lamb Stew

Ingredients:

1 lb, 454g Breast of lamb (cut into 1" pieces)

2oz, 60g Flour.   1/4 litre of water.

1 beef stock cube.   6oz, 175g Mushrooms,

3 Onions, chopped.   3 Carrots (chopped)

3 celery sticks (chopped)   1 lb, 454g Potatoes
                                   (peeled)

Salt and pepper.   2 table spoons of oil.

Method:

Put the potato, celery, mushrooms and carrot in a pot with enough boiling water to cover them. Heat the oil in a large frying pan and brown the meat on all sides. Add the chopped onion and fry until clear. Shake in the flour stirring the meat and onion at the same time and cook for 1-2 minutes over a low heat. Dissolve the stock cube in the water and stir on to the pan, and simmer for 5 minutes. Season to taste. Transfer to the pot with the other vegetables and bring to the boil. Reduce the heat and simmer for about 1 hour or until the meat is tender.

Bacon and Spinach Casserole

Ingredients:

1/2 lb, 220g Cooked bacon (diced) 4oz, 115g Mushrooms.

4oz, 60g Grated cheese.

1/2 lb, 220g diced potato (diced)

1lb,454g Spinach, washed.

2 Eggs.

2 tablespoons Milk.

Salt and pepper.

Method:

Put spinach in a saucepan, cover and simmer for a few minutes in its own moisture. Drain well, chop and season to taste. Place in a casserole dish. Add the diced bacon, potato and mushrooms. Beat the eggs in a bowl, season and add the milk, mix well and pour over the mixture of bacon, mushrooms, potato and spinach. Top with the grated cheese and bake in the oven at 200°C, 400°F, Gas 6 for 30 minutes.

Meat Balls with Tomato Sauce and Mashed Potato.

Ingredients:

1/2 lb 220g Minced beef .

1/2lb 220g Fresh bread crumbs.

2 Onions (finely chopped)

4 Tomatoes (chopped)

2ozs Milk (heated)

3oz, 90mls cold water or stock

3 table spoons of oil.

1 egg (beaten)

3oz 30g Flour.

1lb, 450g Potatoes(peeled)

Salt and pepper.

Method:

Put the mince, bread crumbs, half the chopped onion and beaten egg into a bowl with 2oz of flour and mix well. Shake some flour on to a board and with your hands form the mince into balls. Put some oil on the frying pan and fry the meat balls until brown on all sides. Remove from the pan, put in a casserole dish. Add the chopped onion and fry until soft. Blend in the flour and season to taste. Transfer to the casserole dish add the water and cook in the oven at 200°C, 400°F, Gas 6 for 30 minutes. Put the potatoes in a saucepan of boiling water and simmer for 30 minutes or until cooked. Drain, mash, add the hot milk and butter, mix thoroughly, place in a serving dish and keep hot. Remove the casserole from the oven add the tomatoes and mix in the tomato sauce. Return to the oven for 5 minutes. Serve with mashed potatoes.

Baked Fish with Peas
and New Potatoes

Ingredients:

1lb, 454g Whiting .	1/2lb, 220g Fresh garden peas.
1lb, new Potatoes.	2 table spoons of oil.
1oz, 30g Butter.	1/2 litre of milk.
1 bay leaf.	1/8 teaspoon of nutmeg.
Pepper and salt.	2 teaspoons of corn flour.
Sprig of Parsley (chopped)	

Method:

Place the fish on a lightly greased baking dish, Sprinkle with seasoning and add the bay leaf. Boil the milk and pour over the fish. Cover the dish and bake in the oven at 190°C, 375° F, Gas 5 for 20 minutes. Put the peas in a saucepan cover with water and boil for 15 minutes, drain and put in a serving dish. When the fish is cooked strain the liquid from the fish into a jug, add the corn flour and the chopped parsley. Bring to the boil stirring all the time. Simmer for 1 minute, pour over the fish before serving. Meanwhile, put the potatoes into a pot of boiling water and simmer for 20 minutes or until cooked.

Drain and put in a serving dish. Add a knob of butter and a sprinkling of chopped parsley to the new potatoes and peas. Serve with the fish.

Shepherds Pie

Ingredients:

1 lb Mashed potatoes.

3/4 lb Minced cooked
beef or mutton.

1/4 litre of hot water.

2-3 sticks of celery (chopped)

2 Onions (finely chopped)

1 Beef stock cube.

1 egg, beaten.

4 carrots (chopped)

1 teaspoon of oil.

Method:

Put the meat, onion, celery and carrot in a lightly greased pie dish. Dissolve the stock cube in the hot water and add to the dish. Top with the mashed potato. Ruffle with a fork and brush with the beaten egg. Bake for 15minutes or until brown in a hot oven at 200°C, 400°F, Gas 6,

Dublin Coddle

Ingredients

8 Medium sized potatoes (peeled)

4 Onions (chopped)

8ozs, 220g back rashers (rind on)

8ozs, 220g sausages.

Freshly ground black pepper.

1 tablespoon of chopped parsley.

Method

Put the potatoes into a pot, add the chopped onion then place the rashers and sausages on top. Pour in sufficient cold water to almost cover the ingredients. Bring to the boil, add freshly ground pepper and simmer for about an hour or until cooked. Pour into a serving dish and garnish with the chopped parsley.

Stir Fried Lamb

Ingredients:

1lb, 220g Breast of lamb (cut in strips)

1lb, 454g pasta.   1 tin Tomatoes (chopped)

2 Onions (sliced)   1 clove of garlic (crushed)

1 green pepper
(de-seeded and cut in strips)

2 tablespoons of Oil.

Salt and Freshly ground black pepper.

Method:

Put the pasta into a pot of boiling water, add a teaspoon of oil and simmer for 10 minutes stirring occasionally. When cooked remove from the water, drain, put in a serving dish and keep hot. Put the oil in the wok add the sliced onion and crushed garlic. Fry until clear then add the lamb strips and fry until golden brown. To this add the sliced pepper and the tinned tomato plus the juice and fry for about 5 minutes. Season to taste and pour over the pasta.

Suggestion

When using a bouquet garni
Tie it to the lid or handle of the pot with a piece of string. Then it can be removed easily from the boiling liquid.

Sauces

Bread Sauce

Ingredients:

1/4 litre Milk.	1 Onion.
2ozs, 60g Fresh bread crumbs.	5 Cloves.
1oz Butter.	Salt and pepper.
1/2 Bay leaf.	

Method:

Stick the cloves into the onion and put in a saucepan with the milk and bay leaf. Bring to the boil and simmer for 30 minutes. Remove from the heat, strain and add the bread crumbs and butter. Season to taste.

Mint Sauce

Ingredients:

1 tablespoon of freshly chopped mint.

2 tablespoons of malt vinegar.

2 teaspoons of sugar.

1 tablespoon of boiling water.

Method:

Dissolve the sugar in the boiling water add the mint and vinegar and mix well.

White Sauce

Ingredients:

1/2 litre Milk.   1oz. 30g butter.

1oz, 30g flour.   Salt and pepper

Method:

Melt the butter in a saucepan. Remove from the heat and stir in the flour. Return to the heat and add the milk, stirring all the time. Season to taste and add what ever flavouring or herbs you require. Simmer for 2 minutes and pour into a sauce boat to serve.

Variations of White Sauce:

Add to above: Parsley, Mushrooms, Caper, Egg, Onion, Mustard, Cheese etc.

Apple sauce

Ingredients:

4 Cooking Apples (peeled and sliced)

1oz, 30g Sugar.

Method:

Put the apples in a saucepan and add a couple of teaspoons of water. Stew over a low heat until soft and sugar to taste.

Stuffing

Sage and Onion

Ingredients:

1 Onion (finely chopped)	1oz, 30g Margarine.
4ozs Fresh bread crumbs.	1 teaspoon of dried sage.
1 tablespoon of oil.	Salt and pepper.

Method:

Put some oil on the pan and fry the chopped onion until clear. Put the bread crumbs in a bowl with the onion, sage and margarine. Season to taste, add a little water, and mix well.

Variations of above
Chestnut, Liver, Thyme, Mixed herb, Lemon etc.

Quick salad dressing

Ingredients

3 tablespoons of malt vinegar.

1 tablespoon extra virgin olive oil.

Method

Pour the oil and vinegar into a screw top jar and shake well.

Uses for left over food

Uses for cooked left over potatoes.

1. Make potato cakes.

2. Make colcannon.

3. Use with salads.

4. Fry or roast in the oven.

5. Use for topping.

Potato Cakes.

Ingredients

4oz, 115g Flour.

8ozs, 220g cooked mashed potatoes.

1 teaspoon of baking powder.

2 ozs, 60g butter or margarine.

1 tablespoon of oil.

3ozs Milk.

Method

Sieve together the flour and baking powder into the bowl of mashed potato, add the butter and milk. Mix well to form a dough.Put the dough on a floured board and roll out.Cut into rounds and fry on a lightly oiled pan, turn and fry on the other side until golden brown. Remove to a serving dish and keep hot

Colcannon

Ingredients

6-8 Potatoes (peeled)   1/2 litre of milk.

1 head of green cabbage (shredded)

2ozs, 60g Butter or Margarine (melted)

1 Onion (chopped)

Salt and pepper.

1 tablespoon of parsley (chopped)

Method

Put the potatoes in a pot of boiling water and simmer for 30 minutes or until cooked. Drain, add the milk, mash and keep hot. Cook the cabbage in a pot with as little water as possible, add the chopped onion and boil until tender. Drain and add to the mash. Season to taste and mix well. Put in a serving dish and make a hollow in the centre and pour in the melted butter or margarine.

Did you know?

Starch is a major source of heat and energy and is found in: Rice, Wheat, Oatmeal, Potatoes, Cereals, Bread and Pasta.

Uses for left over meat from the previous meal

Make
Stir-fry, Lasagne, Curry, Stew, Cakes, Sandwiches.

Uses for left over bread

1. Make a delicious sweet.
    Queen of pudding, Summer fruit pudding, Treacle
    pudding or toasted apple pudding
2. Make bread crumbs.
    Use them for stuffing and toppings.
3. Make garlic bread.
    Put some oil on the pan and fry a crushed garlic clove
    until clear. Then fry the sliced bread.

Delicious Sweets

Stuffed Baked Apples

Ingredients:

4 large cooking apples.

3ozs, 50g Sultanas.

1/2 teaspoon of cinnamon.

4 teaspoons golden syrup.

1oz, 30g soft brown sugar.

1oz, 30g Butter.

Method

Remove the cores from the apples. Slit the skin round the centre of each apple to prevent the skin bursting during cooking. Place on a lightly greased baking tray. Mix together the fruit and sugar, stuff the apple centres with the mixture. Pour one teaspoon of syrup over each apple and top with a knob of butter. Bake in a moderate oven 190°C, 375°F, Gas 5 for 40-50 minutes. Serve hot with custard.

Rice Pudding

Ingredients:

I litre of milk.

90g, 3ozs sultanas.

knob butter

4ozs, 115g Short grain rice, (pearl rice)

60g, 2ozs sugar.

Method:

Put the rice and milk in a saucepan, bring to the boil stirring gently, lower the heat and add the sultan and butter, simmer for a few minutes. Transfer to an oven proof dish and cook in a moderate oven at 190°C, 375°F, Gas 5 for 30 minutes. If the rice appears to be too thick add more milk and return to the oven for a further 5 minutes. Serve either hot or cold.

Fresh Fruit Salad

Ingredients:

2 Apples cored and sliced   2 Bananas sliced

12 grapes   2 Pears sliced

2 oranges peeled and segmented   2 tablespoons of honey.

Method

Mix all the fruit together in a serving bowl. Mix the honey with about 1/4 litre warm water. Let it cool, then pour it over the fruit. Serve chilled with cream.

Treacle Pudding

Ingredients:

1/2 lb,230g Bread crumbs.

1/4 lb, 115g Flour.

2 tablespoons of treacle.

1 teaspoon baking powder.

1oz, 30g Butter.

2 Eggs (beaten)

2oz, 60g Brown sugar.

1 Lemon rind (grated)

1/4 litre milk.

Method:

Sift the flour and baking powder into a large bowl. Add the sugar, bread crumbs, grated rind of lemon, beaten eggs and lemon juice. Mix well, then add the treacle and enough milk to moisten the mixture. Spoon into a greased pudding bowl, cover well and steam for 2-3hrs .

Summer Fruit Pudding

Ingredients:

1 lb Fresh soft fruit, Raspberries, Blackcurrants, Strawberries etc.

4 oz, 115g Sugar.

8 Thick slices of bread.

Method:

Use a mixture of fruit or just one fruit. Put the fruit in a saucepan and heat gently for 2-3 minutes stirring all the time but not squashing the fruit. Sugar to taste. Line the base and sides of a lightly greased pudding bowl with the bread. Pour the fruit and juice into the centre of the bowl, cover the top with bread and press down firmly. Place a small plate on top of the bowl, then put it in the oven at180°C, 350°F, Gas 4 for 20 minutes. If you would like to serve it cold, Let it cool before putting into the fridge to chill for a few hours or overnight.

Apple Pie

Ingredients for pastry:

6 oz,175g Flour.

4oz, 115g Margarine.

2 teaspoons of water.

Half teaspoon of Baking Powder

Filling

5-6 cloves.

8 cooking apples.

2 teaspoons of water.

Method:

Sift the flour into a bowl, rub in the margarine. Sprinkle with the water and mix into a dough. Place the dough on a floured board and roll to about 1/4" thick and wide enough to cover the pie dish. Peel and slice 8 cooking apples and put in a saucepan with a couple of teaspoons of water simmer for 5 minutes, sugar to taste. Add the cloves and transfer to the pie dish. Cover with the pastry, seal off the edges and place in a pre- heated 200°C, 400°F, Gas 6 for 30 minutes or until the top is a golden brown colour.

Queen of Puddings

Ingredients:

8ozs, 220g fresh bread crumbs.   3ozs Sultanas.

1 Litre of milk.   2 Eggs

1 tablespoon of sugar.   2 tablespoon of red jam.

1/2 teaspoon of vanilla or lemon essence.

Method:

Put the bread crumbs, dried fruit and sugar in a lightly greased pie dish and mix well. Beat the egg and add to the milk with a few drops of flavouring. Pour over the bread crumb mix. Sprinkle the top with sugar and dot with jam. Bake in the oven at 400°F, 200°C, Gas 6 for 30 minutes. **Serve hot.**

Bread and Butter Pudding

Ingredients:

1/2lb, 230g Stale bread, left over from previous day including heels.

2oz, 60g Butter or margarine.

1/4 litre of milk.

2oz 60g Raisins, Sultanas or mixed fruit.

1 Tablespoon of custard powder.

Method:

Butter the bread, cut it in squares and place in a lightly greased pie dish in layers. Scatter some of the dried fruit between each layer. Put two thirds of the milk in a saucepan to boil, use the other third for dissolving the custard powder which you now add to the boiling milk stirring all the time. Simmer gently for a minute only, add the sugar and pour over the bread in the dish. Place in the pre-heated oven at 200°C, 400°F, Gas 6 and bake for 20 minutes.

Toasted Apple Pudding

Ingredients:

6 thick slices of toast, crusts removed.

2oz, 60g Butter.

1lb, 454g Cooking apples
(cored and sliced)
Finely grated rind and juice of 1 orange.

4ozs, 115g brown
sugar.

1/4 teaspoon of ground cinnamon.

2 Eggs lightly
beaten.

Method:

Mix together the chopped apple, rind and juice of the orange and half the brown sugar in a bowl. Put half of the mixture in the bottom of a lightly greased pie dish. Spread the butter on the toast and slice into strips. Place a layer of buttered toast over the fruit in the dish. Add another layer of fruit, sprinkle with sugar followed by another layer of toast. Mix together the milk, eggs and cinnamon and pour into the dish. Bake in the oven at 200°C, 400°, G 6 for 40 minutes.

Honey Baked Pears

Ingredients:

4 Large pears(cored and halved)

4 desert spoons of clear honey.

1 teaspoon ground cinnamon.

1 oz of oil or butter.

4 cherries.

Method:

Place the pear halves on a lightly greased baking dish. Put one desert spoon of honey on each and place a cherry on top. Put the tray in a pre-heated oven 180°C, 350°, gas 4 and bake for 30 minutes or until the pears are tender. Remove the tray from the oven and cool before serving.

Suggestion

To spoon honey out of a jar,.

Warm a metal spoon over heat or in boiling water.

Bread and Cakes

White Yeast Bread

Ingredients:

1lb, 454g Flour.

1/2 teaspoon of dried yeast.

1/2 teaspoon of sugar.

Luke warm water.

Method:

Put the flour in a mixing bowl and airate by lifting it up with your hands. Add a few drops of the water to the sugar and yeast, mix well and add to 1/4 litre of warm water. Make a hole in the centre of the flour and pour in the yeast. If required add further water to make a stiff dough. Place on a lightly floured baking tray and put in a warm place to rise until it is twice the size (about 2-3 hours) Kneed again and form into the required shape.

Suggestion

To test if a cake is baked:

Insert a skewer into the centre of the cake. If it comes out clean it is fully cooked. If not, return to the oven for a further 10 minutes and check again.

Fluffy Light Brown Bread

Ingredients:

1lb, 454g self raising flour.   2oz, 60g Wheat germ.

2oz, 60g Wheat Bran.   1 teaspoon baking powder

2/3 litre milk.

Method:

Sieve together the flour, wheat germ and baking powder into a large bowl and add the bran. Aerate the mixture by running your fingers through it and lifting it into the air. Add some milk and gradually mix in enough milk to make a light dough. Turn on to a lightly floured baking tray and gently make into a round shape. (Do not kneed) Bake in the oven at 200°C, 400°F, Gas 6 for 45 minutes.

Farmhouse Brown Bread

Ingredients:

1lb, 454g Plain flour.

1/4lb, 115g Wheat germ.

1 litre of butter milk .

1 level teaspoon of salt.

2ozs, 60g wheat bran.

1 level teaspoon of bread soda.

2 Eggs beaten.

Method:

Sieve together the flour, wheat germ, bread soda and salt into a large bowl and add the bran. Whip the beaten egg with some butter milk and add to the mixture. Gradually mix in sufficient butter milk to make a light dough. Turn on to a lightly floured baking tray, gently shape into a round. Place in the oven at 200°C, 400°F, Gas 6 for 45 minutes.

Madeira Cake

Ingredients:

8ozs, 220g Self-raising flour   1/8 litre milk

6ozs, 175g Butter   6ozs, 175g Caster sugar

3 Eggs (lightly beaten)

Method:

Line and lightly grease a 6" cake tin. Cream the butter and the sugar until light and fluffy. Gradually beat in the eggs , fold in the flour and add enough milk to make a soft consistency. Spoon the mixture into the prepared tin and place in the oven. Bake at 180°C, 350°F, Gas 4 for 1 1/2 hours. Remove from oven, insert a skewer into the centre and if it comes out clean it is cooked. Leave in the tin for 10 minutes before transferring to a wire rack to cool.

Raspberry Buns

Ingredients:

8ozs, 220g plain flour.	3ozs, 130g Margarine.
2 Eggs (beaten)	2 level teaspoons baking powder.
1/2 teaspoon salt.	2oz, 60g Sugar.
2 tablespoons of Jam.	Milk to mix.

Method:

Pre heat oven to 200°, 400°F. Mark 6. Sieve together flour, baking powder and salt into a bowl, rub in the margarine, add the beaten eggs and the sugar with a little milk to make a dough. Divide the dough into balls by rolling it in the palms of your hands. Press a hole in the centre of each ball. Fill with raspberry jam and place on a lightly greased baking tray. Bake in the oven for 20 minutes or until cooked.

Victoria Sandwich

Ingredients:

4oz, 115g Plain flour.	2 Eggs.
4oz, 115g Butter.	1 teaspoon of baking powder.
4oz, 115g Sugar.	Vanilla essence.
1/2 teaspoon salt.	

Method:

Pre heat oven to 200°C, 400°F Mark 6. Sieve together the flour, baking powder and salt. Cream together the butter and sugar in a large bowl. Blend in the eggs one at a time with a little of the flour and a drop of the vanilla essence, fold in the remaining flour and add a little milk if necessary to make a soft batter. Turn the mixture into two lightly greased sandwich tins and bake in the oven for 20 minutes. When done remove from the oven and sandwich the cake together with jam.

Fruit Cake

Ingredients:

8oz, 220g Self-raising Flour.

4oz, 115g Caster sugar.

6oz, 115g Mixed fruit.

4oz, 115g Margarine.

2 Eggs, lightly beaten.

2oz, 60g Glace cherries, sliced

Method:

Line and grease a 7" cake tin. Cream the margarine with the sugar and eggs. Gradually add the dried fruit with some flour gently mixing all the time, fold the remaining flour into the creamed mixture. Spoon the mixture into the lined tin, Keeping the top even, Bake in a moderate oven 220°C, 355°F, Gas 4 for 1 hour and 15 minutes or until baked. Remove from the oven, leave to cool in the tin for about 10 minutes before removing, then turn out on to a wire rack to cool.

Cherry Buns

Ingredients:

8oz, 220g Self-raising flour.   2 Eggs.

3ozs, 90g Margarine.   4ozs, 115g Sugar.

4ozs, 115g Glace cherries (halved)   1/4 litre Milk.

1 teaspoon baking powder.

Method:

Sieve the flour and baking powder into a bowl and add the cherries. Cream the margarine and sugar and blend in the eggs and half of the milk. Pour into the bowl of flour and mix well to a soft consistency add more of the milk if required. Lightly grease a bun tray and three quarter fill each section with the mixture. Bake in a pre-heated oven 200°C, 400°F, Gas 6 for 20 minutes or until risen and are a golden brown colour.

Soda Bread

Ingredients:

1lb, 454g Plain flour.

1/2 teaspoon salt.

1/2 teaspoon of bread soda.

1/2 litre Butter milk.

Method:

Sieve the flour, salt and bread soda into a large bowl. Gradually add the butter milk and gently mix to form a soft dough. Turn out on to a floured baking tray, gently form into a round shape. Place in the oven. Bake at 240° c, 475°F gas 7 for 40 minutes.

Swiss roll

Ingredients:

3oz, 90g plain flour.

3 Eggs (beaten)

Caster sugar for dusting.

1/2 teaspoon baking powder.

3ozs Caster sugar.

4 Desert spoons of warm jam.

Method:

Sieve the flower and baking powder together and put in a warm place Blend the eggs and sugar together until thick and creamy . Fold in the warm flour and beat with a whisk until smooth. Turn at once on to the lightly greased baking tray and spread evenly. Place in the pre-heated oven and bake for 15 minutes or until cooked. Remove from the oven, loosen the edges and turn immediately on to a piece of grease proof paper dusted with caster sugar. Spread the warm jam on the cake and roll up at once. Leave to cool before slicing.

Jam

Rosemary's Tips when making Jam

1. Before you start to make jam: Collect the required amount of jars and wash them thoroughly.

2. Put the jars in a hot oven for about 10 minutes. Then turn off the oven and leave for a while to cool slightly before putting the jam into them.

3. The fruit you are using, should be dry and fresh. If not the jam will become mouldy.

4. The setting time varies with the fruit used. To test, pour a teaspoonful on to a plate. If it sets when cold the jam is done.

5. Too little boiling gives a thin jam, too much boiling spoils the colour.

6. When the jars are sealed, store them upside down.

Raspberry Jam

Ingredients:

4lb, 1700g Raspberries (stems removed)

4lb, 1700g Sugar.

2 teaspoons water.

Method:

Put sugar into a bowl and place in a warm oven to heat for a few minutes. Put two teaspoons of water into a preserving pan or large saucepan add the raspberries and heat slowly until the juices begin to flow, Increase the heat and simmer gently until the fruit becomes soft stirring all the time. Add the heated sugar stir until it is dissolved, then bring to the boil and simmer gently for 5 minutes. Do the teaspoon test to see if it is set. Remove from the heat, and let it stand for 5 minutes then stir and pot. Top with waxed paper discs straight away, let it cool before sealing jars.

Gooseberry Jam

Ingredients:

4lbs.1700g Gooseberries (topped and tailed)

4lbs,1700g Sugar.

4 cups of water.

Method

Put the sugar in a bowl and place it in a warm oven to heat for a few minutes. Put the gooseberries and water into a preserving pan or heavy saucepan and boil for a few minutes stirring occasionally until the fruit is soft.Add the sugar and bring to the boil. Simmer gently for about 5 minutes stirring all the time, until when a teaspoon test sets. Remove from the heat and let it stand for 5 minutes. Stir and pot immediately. Top with waxed paper discs and leave to cool before sealing the jars.

Blackcurrant Jam

Ingredients:

4 lbs, 1700g Blackcurrants (topped and tailed)

4 lbs, 1700g Sugar.

1 cup of water.

Method:

Put the sugar in a bowl and place in a warm oven to heat for a few minutes. Put the fruit into a preserving pan or large saucepan. Add the water and boil for a few minutes stirring occasionally until the fruit is soft. Add the sugar and simmer gently for about 5 minutes stirring all the time. Do the teaspoon test and if it sets it is done. Remove from the heat and let it stand for a few minutes. Stir and pot immediately. Top with wax paper discs and leave to cool before sealing the jars.

Strawberry Jam

Ingredients:

4 lbs, 1700g Strawberries, stems removed.

4 lbs,1700g Sugar.

Method:

Put the sugar in a bowl and place it in a warm oven to heat for a few minutes. Put the strawberries into a preserving pan or heavy large saucepan. Heat very gently until the juice starts to flow, stirring occasionally. Add the sugar and stir until dissolved. Then gradually turn up the heat and simmer gently for about 5 minutes. Do the teaspoon test and see if it sets, If not return to the heat and boil for another 5 minutes. Remove from the heat and let it stand for a few minutes. Stir and pot immediately. Top with wax paper discs and leave to cool before sealing.

Rosemary's tips to reduce the cost of running a household

1. Turn down the temperature of the central heating.

2. Turn off lights when you are not in the room.

3. Encourage the family to walk or cycle instead of using the car.

4. Save water. Fix dripping taps. It may be only a washer you need.

5. Encourage the family to have showers as they use less water than baths.

6. Use half the amount of shower gel when taking a shower, The surplus is only washed down the plug hole.

7. Reduce the amount of washing powder or liquid when washing .Use your washing machine, dish washer and dryer less frequently.

8. Only use the electric fire if you have to.

9. When lighting fires use rolled up newspaper underneath the logs or coal.

10. Lag the hot water cylinder.

11. Cut down on phone calls. Text rather than call.

12. When cleaning windows or mirrors use scrunched up newspaper to shine the glass as it leaves a lovely shine.

13. Use vinegar and bread soda for cleaning showers, hand basins, baths etc.

14. Have a pot of mixed herbs of your choice on the kitchen window sill.

15. Use cereal box liners as freezing bags and bread wrappers to cover food in the fridge.

16. Could you cut back on alcohol or smoking?

Do you know the following numbers?

HSE National Information line   Callsave 1850 24 1850

Social Welfare Office   Lo Call 1890 66 22 44

Garda Confidential line   Freefone 1800666111

Emergency calls
(Fire, Ambulance, Doctor)   Tel No 999 or 112

Taking care of your clothes

Take some time every day to put clothes away in good order.
Make some time available for removing stains and ironing.
Clean collars and neck-lines marked with make up with a
grease solvent. Replace buttons and do the odd repair before
clothes are put away. Always hang clothes up immediately
after wearing and close all fastenings as you do so. If your
clothes brush is leaving fluff behind. Wind a piece of sellotape
with the sticky side out around your hand and dab the garment.

Authors Tips for Christmas Presents

Make hampers with fruit and preserves, or buy things like
books and toys, one at a time each week throughout the year.

Dealing with stains

Scorches and burns:- Sponge with a solution of 2 tablespoons of borax to 1/2 litre of warm water.(Wash if washable)

Oil, grease, tar or paint:- Sponge with turpentine, rinse and then wash.(If washable)

Alcohol:- Blot immediately, rinse in cold water and wash.(If washable)

Milk and Eggs:- Rinse in cold water straight away. If washable wash.

Tea and coffee:- If washable, wash in a solution of 2 tablespoons of borax to 1/2 litre of warm water.

Ball-point pen Ink:- Dab with a cloth dampened with methylated spirits. Wash if washable.

Blood:- Rinse in cold water straight away, then wash if washable.

Chewing gum:- Freeze and when frozen it will lift off.